The Young Woman's Guide to Older Men

Is An Age Difference Relationship Right For You?

Wayne & Tamara Mitchell

Third Ghost Press

Copyright ©2023 by Wayne and Tamara Mitchell

Ebook ISBN: 978-1-948158-16-9

Paperback ISBN: 978-1-948158-17-6

Cover photo: ©Can Stock Photo / nikdoorg

All rights reserved.

No portion of this book may be reproduced in any form without written permission from the publisher or author, except as permitted by U.S. copyright law. No liability is assumed for losses or damages due to the information provided. You are responsible for your own choices, actions, and results. For privacy reasons, some names and details were changed.

Portions of this book were previously published in *Age Difference Relationships*.

Published by Third Ghost Press, PO Box 3003, Springfield Missouri 65808.

Visit the authors' website at: www.WayneAndTamara.com

Contents

Epigraph	V
1. Introduction	1
2. Getting Down to Basics	3
3. Need or Neediness	5
4. What A Ride It Was	9
5. Why?	15
6. Love Is Common, True love Is Rare	19
7. The One Thing They Talk About	21
8. The Camel's Nose	25
9. The Ages of a Woman	27
10. How Now Brown Cow	29
11. You've Got Daddy Issues, Darling	33

12.	Numbers	35
13.	Out of Bounds	39
14.	Crushes	43
15.	The Heart of The Matter	49
16.	The Ideal Age Difference	57
17.	Voices of Success	61
18.	Should I Go Forward?	67
19.	How to Tell Family and Friends	81
20.	Another Word About Telling	87
21.	Stages of Life	93
22.	Three Principles	101
23.	Hard Work	105
24.	A Scale	109
25.	Summing Up	111
About Wayne & Tamara		113
Acknowledgments		115
Endnotes		117

"Men's courses will foreshadow certain ends, to which, if persevered in, they must end. But if the courses be departed from, the ends will change."

—Charles Dickens, *A Christmas Carol*

Chapter One

Introduction

If you're a woman wondering if you should go out with, date, or marry an older man, this book is for you.

When we began writing, we were thinking of women from their teens to their 30s. But most of what we say applies to any woman significantly younger than her partner.

One thing you should know up front is that we are an age difference couple. Wayne is over 18 years older than Tamara, and we married when Tamara was 33. Both of us had been married before. We know many readers will be younger than Tamara, and some will be older.

Many psychologists claim that the first blush of love fades as couples come to see the other person for the imperfect person they are. Except it didn't happen that way for us.

WAYNE & TAMARA MITCHELL

We still see ourselves as perfect for each other, and we've been married 26 years. We can't give you our experience or guarantee how your life will turn out. But we can tell you our experience exists. And we can offer ways to think about your own age gap relationship.

By a quirk of fate, a few years after we married, we were invited to write a newspaper advice column. We did that for 22 years. During that time, we received tens of thousands of letters. In this book, we share some of those real-life stories, as well as results of scientific studies.

Loads of books tell you how to "build" a relationship and make it "work." They range from Gary Chapman's five love languages to John Gottman's seven principles. Though you may find some useful things in those books, this is not that kind of book. This book is about your heart.

If you're looking for your own personal yes or no, we want you to feel more confident in your decision—whether you go ahead, pull back, or end the relationship. This decision will influence the rest of your life. Ultimately, only you can decide.

Chapter Two

Getting Down to Basics

When Robinson Crusoe found himself shipwrecked on a deserted island, he cried in despair. "Oh, that there had been but one soul saved out of this ship, that I might have had one companion to converse with!"

We are alone in the universe. To share our space with another human being—that's what a relationship is about. One self meeting another self. With the right person, we are no longer single. With the wrong person, we feel even more alone.

Chesterton wrote, "There are no words to express the abyss between isolation and having one ally. It may be conceded to the mathematician that four is twice two. But two is not twice one; two is two thousand times one."

Alex Newton, who tracks such things, says that Romance is by far the most popular genre in fiction. At last count, he tallied roughly a hundred subcategories in the Romance field. The books range from high literature, like Jane Austen, to mass market paperbacks and ebooks.

Wherever these books land on the spectrum, they point to our most basic need. Love.

There is nothing trivial about your desire to be loved. It is a timeless story, far older than *Pride and Prejudice,* and more current than last year's bestseller.

The main point in this chapter

Our aloneness is the first thing relationships are about. The second thing is love.

Chapter Three

Need or Neediness

You are a woman. A female self. You are drawn to men. A male self. It is your need. It is not the need of all women, but it is your need.

But need is not neediness. Neediness is the desperate desire for love. That makes the needy person subordinate. Even worse, neediness impairs judgment.

Neediness is a poverty of self. It is the desire to cling. A needy person is empty and wants someone else to fill them up. That has little chance of satisfying. We must fill ourselves up first.

That's why Elizabeth Barrett Browning wrote, "I love thee to the level of each day's most quiet need." She did not write "I love thee to the level of my neediness."

WAYNE & TAMARA MITCHELL

Love is about need. I am a woman. I need a man. It is in me to want. The problem is, not just any man will do.

A woman writes:

I have been scouring your website looking for a piece of consolation, but I am so heartbroken I felt the need to write you guys myself.

I am a 21-year-old woman devoted to saving a relationship with a 31-year-old abusive, bipolar, unfaithful, commitment-phobic man-child, who I wish I wasn't deeply in love with, because it would be so damn much easier.

We have been living together for a year and a half and together three years. I must say he is a Freudian nightmare in the sense that he has as many issues as anyone I've ever met.

He claims he is madly in love with me, and he says even if I were a paraplegic, he would stay by my side because he loves who I am so much. He wants marriage, kids, et cetera. However, his drinking (or rather his behavior when he drinks, which is every night) has caused so many problems between us.

Though he cut down considerably since we met, for the sake of saving the relationship, he still ends up drunk and belligerent every night and spews out the most mean, negative, and blatantly hurtful things from his mouth.

THE YOUNG WOMAN'S GUIDE TO OLDER MEN

He tells me sex and love are two completely separate things, and he does not feel strong enough to stay faithful to me. Although he swears he wants nothing more than to be true to me, he keeps making the argument that men have been programmed to spread their seed and this natural urge is a part of their physical appetite and has nothing to do with the person they love.

He says he cannot help it and cannot promise to stay faithful, but he expects me to be fine with it and stay faithful to him.

He says these things frequently when he is drunk, almost like he is getting off on the power trip that comes with watching me cry, while loving every minute of it. When he wakes up, he claims not to recall saying these things. I keep wondering if the alcohol is acting as a truth serum or making him say things he doesn't mean.

Either way, I cannot go on this way. It has to stop, or I cannot stay, though the thought of leaving him would shatter my heart into a zillion pieces.

I already caught him cheating once and took him back, though it shredded all my dignity. I threw all my own morals and ethics out the window and forgave him, because I thought he was genuinely sorry, and he swore it would never happen again.

Beyond that, I am so loyal and need to be with someone who appreciates that loyalty and gives it back to me with an open and loving heart.

I feel unattractive to him, though we have a good sex life, and I am a professional print and clothing model. Every day I find myself trying to pick pieces of my self-esteem off the floor, that he had so much fun obliterating.

If I were someone else reading this very email, I would think the girl writing was so stupid for not already leaving that I would delete it and laugh.

Gigi

Gigi's letter is not an age difference letter, because the age gap is incidental. Despite what she believes, her letter is not about love. It's about neediness, and probably the loveless, chaotic background she comes from.

You cannot settle on a life partner simply because he's who you bump into every day.

The main point in this chapter

Love is about need, not about neediness.

The second most important point

If you act from neediness, you're apt to end up with the wrong man.

Chapter Four

What A Ride It Was

But what does the right man look like? Let's give you an example.

A woman told us...

When I was 21, I was introduced to a man of 45 by mutual friends. It was a chance meeting, where we all happened to be at the same place at the same time. I was talking to a couple I'd known for a while when my husband-to-be happened along.

His full-time job was school principal. He was divorced; I had never been married.

Well, they introduced us, and we decided to go across the street for a drink. After a couple of drinks, my husband-to-be invited us to his house to visit awhile. While there, he took me on a tour of the house, and as we moved from room to room, he asked if he could call me sometime.

I said, "Yes," thinking I'd never hear from him again. Later, we all left, and I was quite surprised to get a call from him 10 days later. He asked me out to dinner and I accepted.

He had two children. One was grown and out of the house. In fact, his son was four months older than I, and his daughter was three years younger. We actually took his daughter on a few dinner dates. She and I hit it off right away, and she gave her dad a "thumbs up" about our dating. I didn't meet the son until some months later, as he was in the army. We also hit it off.

We dated for eight months. Every so often, he'd say, "I wish I could ask you to marry me." He didn't feel it was fair for me since he'd had a vasectomy during his first marriage and he figured the day would come when I would want children.

By that time, I already had some major "female problems," and my family doctor told me I would have a difficult time ever getting pregnant, if at all, so I hadn't had my heart set on children anyway.

There was a great love between us. I was a mature 21, not some giggly, goofy airhead, and I am also smart. He happened to like smart women. I was no great beauty, but I was nice looking. My husband described me as a "handsome" woman.

THE YOUNG WOMAN'S GUIDE TO OLDER MEN

When he once more stated he wished he could ask me to marry him, after seven months of dating, I looked at him and said, "Well, why don't you, then?"

He looked at me and said, "Will you?"

I said, "Yes, I will."

That was on July 27th, and on September 1st we were married. We decided one Sunday to get married the next Sunday. I went to see our pastor, and he set the whole thing up with the help of my ex-boyfriend's mother (who was also at the wedding with her husband).

It was a small wedding in church at 8:00 p.m. on a Sunday evening with 30 friends in attendance. NO relatives. My best friend's dad gave me away in proxy for my dad. My folks couldn't get away as they were over 700 miles away and in the middle of harvest, but they gave their blessing.

We were VERY happily married for 20 years until his untimely death from an aortal aneurism. There was not ONE day of regret for either of us. I have a terrific relationship with his kids to this day.

I also don't regret not having kids. A hysterectomy in my 30s was conclusive proof there would never have been any children for me anyway.

His friends were more against the marriage than mine were. But after meeting and socializing with them, his friends were wont to say that we had the "perfect" marriage. I don't know about perfect, but it was darn good.

The communication was great, the sex was even better, and there was SO much laughter in our home since I am something of a wit and he was something of a character. While not particularly funny himself, he certainly appreciated and understood wit in others.

Every evening, we'd come home from work, and whoever got home first would put on a pot of coffee. When the other one got home, we'd plop down at the kitchen table and gab over coffee for an hour.

As a school principal, he had some doozy stories to tell, and I worked with people who also provided highly amusing material. We never tired of conversation, and I can count the fights we had on one hand and still have fingers left over.

He was the greatest guy on the face of the earth, as far as I'm concerned. They say women marry their fathers, but, for some reason, I married my mother. It is to laugh—how much alike they were. Both were reserved, but with laughs so infectious and bubbling, it burst out of them like a geyser erupting.

I have now been a widow as long as I was married. I've never dated another man, never been interested in dating another man, and will probably NEVER date another man. His memory is more than enough for me. I've seen what a can of worms second marriages can open when you've been intensely happy the first time.

THE YOUNG WOMAN'S GUIDE TO OLDER MEN

I saw it with my mother, and I will NEVER put myself in that position. I am quite content with my dog and cats for company and visits with my family. We are all close.

His parents accepted me once they got to know me. I didn't meet them until AFTER we were married.

His dad accused him of robbing the cradle, but once his folks got to know me, I think they thought he'd done pretty well for himself. Winning over his dad was considered something of a "coup" by other family members.

His mother was something of a character herself. She was brilliant and talented in many ways and had an absolutely wicked wit. What laughs we had.

My husband and I shared the same taste in music. Both of us LOVED to dance (he was fabulous at it), and we shared the same worldview. He hadn't known what affection was before meeting me, so I had to teach him. He was an apt pupil.

His kids couldn't get over the difference in him, and were thrilled with it because it spilled over into his relationships with them. It also made him a much happier man. He told me his years with me were the happiest of his whole life. He hadn't laughed enough, so it thrilled my soul to be able to bring out that part of him.

What a ride it was. I thank God that He brought us together. My only regret is that he didn't live longer, but the years we had were enough to last me the rest of my life. Dr. Laura would probably shit nickels about the whole situation, but she's not ALWAYS right, and what was right for us may not be right for somebody else. It's who he was and who I was that made it work.

If there were ever two people who completed two halves of a whole, it was us. We forgot about the age difference and just LOVED each other. There was NEVER a day that went by when we didn't say, "I love you," to one another. Mostly, it was several times a day. When you say it, you believe it, and when you believe it, you act like it. It's great reinforcement and the marriage doesn't deteriorate into grunts passing for communication.

There was also a LOT of hugging and kissing, just because we LIKED it. Once he understood true affection (as opposed to sex), he became a MASTER at it. He could thank my parents for teaching it to me, so I had it to pass on to him.

Jan

You might be younger or older than Jan was. You might be hip, urban, conservative, or rural. It doesn't matter. This is what true love looks like.

The main point in this chapter

The best guide to finding the right man is understanding what genuine love looks like.

Chapter Five

Why?

In all known human societies, past and present, husbands are older than their wives. Not in all cases, but on average. What is true of wives and husbands is true in relationships generally.[1]

Why is the man usually older? One explanation is girls mature faster than boys.[2] They enter puberty about two years earlier, and their activities are closer to their adult roles than boys' activities are.

Another explanation is the difference results from societal norms.[3] That may explain why the age gap varies from society to society. But it does not explain why the age difference is found across all cultures, continents, religions, forms of government, ethnic backgrounds, and social rules.[4]

Evidence for the male-older age gap is found throughout recorded history. What's more, remote peoples living today—people who still live in primitive ways—show the same trend.

There is a more plausible explanation for the age gap.

When we were a small, fragile species, struggling to exist, reproduction was everything. Like all species, we were in a race against the death rate. Ninety-nine percent of all species who ever lived have lost that race. In fact, we almost lost that race ourselves.[5]

In this story, a woman would want an older man because he is likely to bring more provisions she can use for her (and her children's) survival. An older man is likely to have more resources than a younger one, and a younger man's potential is harder to assess.

Males also select for survival. They instinctively value youth and beauty in women, which correlates with reproductive potential.[6]

As evolutionary psychologist David Buss says, each of us is a descendant of two people who successfully reproduced, and those people, our parents, are at the end of thousands of generations who successfully reproduced.[7] As Buss writes, "Our mating mechanisms are the living fossils that reveal who we are and where we come from."[8]

THE YOUNG WOMAN'S GUIDE TO OLDER MEN

That's not the entire story, of course. Other things are involved in picking a partner, things like kindness, ambition, intelligence, and a sense of humor.

But people take a long time to grow up. That means parents, especially women, must invest a lot in the young. They will often seek men with resources. And since a man's reproductive ability declines more slowly than a woman's, there is no disadvantage in marrying an older man.

We navigate between two worlds, one seen and one unseen. The first world is a world of love, romance, and feelings. The second world is an ancient world shaped by our biology. It operates mostly below our conscious notice.

The main point in this chapter

Our biology points women toward older men and men toward younger women. These two tendencies, by themselves, have nothing to do with love.

CHAPTER SIX

Love Is Common, True love Is Rare

David Buss, the evolutionary psychologist, is a rigorous scientist. He's spent his life studying the connection between women and men. His work has brought him into contact with the bright side of romantic relationships, as well as with the dark side—stalking and sexual exploitation.

He knows about the supposed "stages" of love—attraction, infatuation, romanticizing, sex, commitment, and falling out of love.

A few years ago, he and other eminent scientists were asked a simple question. "What do you believe is true even though you cannot prove it?"

Buss said he believes in true love. He also said he believes most people don't have it.

True love, he said, "...knows no fences, has no barriers or boundaries. It's difficult to define, eludes modern measurement, and seems scientifically wooly. But I know true love exists. I just can't prove it."[1]

We agree with David Buss.

The main point in this chapter

Love is common, true love is rare.

The second most important point

Many psychologists and therapists writing about relationships are not writing about love. They write about living together with less friction and more consideration.

Chapter Seven

The One Thing They Talk About

One summer, psychologist Caryl Rusbult drove across the United States with a companion. Somewhere in the Arizona desert, her travel companion asked a question. "Tell me why," he said, "people stick with their partner."[1]

Rusbult then summarized all the research on the subject, mentioning things like compatibility and the role of physical appearance.

Hundreds of miles later, when Rusbult finished talking, her companion said, "Okay, but can you tell me why people stick with their partner?"

A lot of psychological research, though interesting, fumbles this basic question.

One suggestive study looked at couples who had been together for decades, yet were still intensely in love.[2] When researchers scanned their brains, fMRI brain scans confirmed what the couples said.

The researchers wrote, "Overall, results suggest that for some individuals the reward-value associated with a long-term partner may be sustained, similar to new love, but also involves brain systems implicated in attachment and pair-bonding." The scientists also observed that this may cause "some distress for those in satisfying, but not intensely in love marriages."

Some psychologists have a hard time explaining these couples; others deny they exist. But we believe the reason some couples stay deeply connected is far more subtle than the usual explanations in relationship books.

In the letters we receive from people who clearly belong together, the writers do not focus on relationship building or learning communication skills.

Instead, they talk about something else. The *connection* they have. When they speak to us, it is clear their connection is not a conscious decision, nor about making a choice.

Which brings up the topic in the next chapter. The lack of connection.

THE YOUNG WOMAN'S GUIDE TO OLDER MEN

The main point in this chapter

Some couples stay deeply in love throughout their lives.

Chapter Eight

The Camel's Nose

I am utterly infatuated with an older man. He's already been married. He happens to work at a bar I visit with friends. After bumping into him a few times on his nights off around town, and having some brilliant (though admittedly inebriated) conversations, and realizing how lovely and gorgeous he is, I asked him his age. Expecting a maximum of 28, I was shocked when he said 35. Our attraction is mutual, and he was just as shocked to hear I am 20.

We didn't mention age again, and I haven't seen him since. I am nearing the end of a degree and cannot stop thinking about him and the ridiculous possibility of a relationship in the future. I wonder if this large age difference can prevent two people having anything more than just a good time. Is this destined to end in tears?

Savannah

Savannah, there is a logical fallacy called the camel's nose. It refers to the argument that one shouldn't permit one event because it will inevitably lead to a later, undesirable event. In other words, if you allow the camel to put his nose in your tent, the rest of the camel will likely follow.

As a matter of logic, the argument is weak. However, emotions have their own logic. Once a woman is physically intimate with a man, she will consider this a relationship. A relationship that may lead to marriage. Women often stay with an unsuitable mate, because they were intimate.

If you feel all you would get from this man is his nose under your tent, choose another camel.

Wayne & Tamara

This leads to the point of the next chapter.

The main point in this chapter

If you let the wrong camel stick his nose under your tent, you're likely to end up with the wrong camel.

Chapter Nine

The Ages of a Woman

A woman's life has three ages.

In the first, her parents are at the center.

In the second, her peers are at the center.

In the third, she's at the center. She's an adult, capable of making her own decisions.

But near the end of adolescence, nothing says you've entered adulthood. There is no finish line. The boundary between adolescence and adulthood is invisible.

As Leah Somerville, of Harvard's Center for Brain Science, observes, maturity does not come to us all at once—it comes in waves.[1] That's why sorting things out when you're emerging as an adult is hard.

There is a second complication. Nearly all of us believe we are the exception to the rule. Because we don't want to feel vulnerable, we think, "It couldn't happen to me." Even though it could.

That's why we think other people are more likely than us to face divorce, skin cancer, heart attack, tooth decay, mugging, unwanted pregnancy, food poisoning, and an auto accident while on the phone.[2]

The main point in this chapter

The age at which a woman becomes an adult, capable of making her own decisions, is hard to gauge.

Chapter Ten

How Now Brown Cow

Online dating sites, personal ads, and male and female preference surveys across countries show the same trend. Usually, the man is a little older.

On most continents, males vary from about two years older than their partner to somewhat over three years older.[1] In Norway, for example, the average age gap at first marriage is 1.9 years, while in Greece it is 3.6 years. Most other countries fall somewhere in between.[2]

In the United States, over a third of married couples are within a year of each other. Sixty percent are within 2-3 years, and 75% within 5 years of each other.[3]

Imagine a pasture with a 100 cows. Seventy-five cows are large, black and white Holsteins. Twenty-five are small, caramel-colored Scottish Highlanders.

If you are a woman with an older man, and your age gap is over 5 years, you're in a 25% minority. That can be a problem. Things outside the norm garner attention, and attention is often a negative. In the eyes of many, it means you do not fit.[4]

If you are a young woman in a gap relationship greater than 9 years, you're in a 10% minority. If your partner is 10 or more years older, you're in a 7% minority, or less. That will put a spotlight on you as a couple.

A man writes about his younger wife…

I have been married for almost a year to my wife, who is 22 years younger than me. I'm 47. Lately she's been saying that she's more self-conscious about being with me in public, and this did not bother her before.

She has been acting distant and says she feels the need to be "independent," or at least appear to be "older," so we will not attract attention in public. I love her dearly and have told her on many occasions I do not care what the public thinks, but will honor her concerns. I try to stay distant while we walk in public and try not to use terms that are endearing.

I feel a bit distressed and hurt that she is now taking me for the "older" man, and she is more concerned about what society thinks than what we mean to each other. We dated

THE YOUNG WOMAN'S GUIDE TO OLDER MEN

for five years before we got married. Both our families are supportive of our marriage, and I get along well with her family.

Is there something I can do to help her understand that love and companionship are what I'm concerned with and try to get her focused on this, too? Is there something else she is not telling me that I'm missing?

John

We told John:

Your wife at 18 or 19 was flattered by your interest. There is a certain cachet for a young woman in catching the eye of a mature man. It tells her she is truly a grown woman. But at 25, her view has changed; she is envious of the life she doesn't have.

As a young female, she may have thought men her own age were immature boys. But now, grown up, she may regret her youthful arrogance.

There is a vast difference between an 18-year-old and a 25-year-old. If she was 25 when you met, it might have been different. She would give less weight to what others think and more weight to what she thinks and feels. Perhaps you gave her credit for a maturity she didn't possess.

We imagine things will not get better. Even if she loves you, the harsh spotlight may be too much. She is pushing you away, and it's a distance likely to grow.

The main point in this chapter

Larger than average age gaps can attract attention, often negative attention.

Chapter Eleven

You've Got Daddy Issues, Darling

Sometimes women with older men are accused of having "daddy issues." It's a way to dismiss their feelings.

But is it true?

Two researchers, Sara Skentelbery and Darren Fowler, put the daddy-issue question to a test.[1] They designed a scientific study comparing two groups of women. In the first group, the women were more than 17 years younger than their partner; in the second group, the women were 1.2 years younger.

Skentelbery and Fowler reported that, "There was no relationship found between magnitude of age difference in partners and scores for relationship satisfaction, thus, the age discrepancy in one's relationship cannot predict happiness in the relationship." They also found no significant difference in attachment styles between the two groups.

Rather than having "daddy issues," which means the relationship is a bit twisted, larger age gaps probably reflect no more than the normal variability in the human population. We are not all alike.

The main point in this chapter

There is no obvious connection between age gap and happiness.

Chapter Twelve

Numbers

The absolute value of a number is its distance from zero on a number line.

But age in relationships does not follow absolute value. Take the number 6. A 6 is a 6, but at 15 and 21 the age difference is too much. At 25 and 31, the difference matters much less, and at 45 and 51, no one gives it a second thought.

Age in relationships follows a sliding scale. Plug in two numbers, like 12 and 20. Nope, doesn't work. Plug in 40 and 48, and who cares? Age in relationships is about maturity.

A 14-year-old cannot sign a contract, join the military, get a tattoo, drive a car, or freely drink alcohol. Children are protected from certain activities by law. And if they commit a crime, the law may protect them from being treated as an adult.

Why? Because they lack maturity.

Maturity implies the ability to prioritize, make life decisions, and face the challenges of adult life.

The American Academy of Child and Adolescent Psychiatry (AACAP) puts the matter this way. "Adolescents differ from adults in the way they behave, solve problems, and make decisions. There is a biological explanation for this difference."[1]

According to AACAP, the difference is that adolescents act from the brain's amygdala, the area responsible for immediate reactions, not the frontal cortex, the brain area responsible for reasoning. As a result, adolescents act on impulse, engage in risky behavior, and misread social cues and emotions. Their adult brain, the more rational brain, is not fully developed.

Once we learn the times tables, we can multiply for the rest of our life. Maturity is like that. It enables us to move forward with the best chance of success.

Children gain experience with balls when they are young. They learn how to handle a soccer ball, a basketball, or a baseball. They are experienced ball handlers. Though they are warned not to play with a ball inside the house, they may toss one around until a lamp breaks.

In the same way, 16-year-olds are allowed to drive automobiles, even though their brains won't be fully developed until they are 25. Some 16-year-olds drive well; many do not. The difference is in their level of maturity.

The main point in this chapter

Age in romantic relationships follows a sliding scale.

The second most important point

Maturity involves awareness of consequences. It implies the ability to act from a basis deeper than the emotion of the moment.

Chapter Thirteen

Out of Bounds

The age of the younger partner matters.

A young teen writes:

Hi, my name is Kimberly and I'm 13. I need some advice about a situation I'm in. Okay, here goes. My boyfriend is 18 and I really do love him. I know he's too old for me, but he loves me too. I know a lot of adults will say he wants me for sex, but it's not true. The topic of sex never even came up until I brought it up.

I am mature for my age, in appearance and mentality. We tried to have sex once, but we couldn't because his little sisters interrupted. I do plan to have sex with him. There is no doubt in my mind he is the person I was meant to be with.

I have had many other boyfriends, and I know the difference between love and a crush.

Kimberly

At 13, Kimberly lacks the maturity to understand how her life is unfolding.

The very young don't have experience with jobs and layoffs, cars and insurance, taxes and electric bills. They don't know the cost of groceries. They can picture a wedding but not their life afterward. And they may think a midnight curfew is a problem!

The other issue with the young is that they are easily exploited.

There's this guy I've been talking to. He was a friend of some friends. We were introduced, and we clicked instantly. He's the sweetest guy I've ever met. He tells me I'm beautiful and that I have the voice of an angel. Yesterday, he asked if he could have my heart.

The only thing is that he's 38 and I'm 17. I don't care how old he is. He knows how old I am, and he doesn't have a problem with it. I'm a little worried if we pursue a relationship, he'll get in trouble. He is in law enforcement but so is my father, so we are both aware what could happen if anyone found out, but he doesn't seem to care about that.

I'm so confused right now. What should I do?

Penny

THE YOUNG WOMAN'S GUIDE TO OLDER MEN

At 17, Penny is bowled over by the poetry of the words. *You have the voice of an angel. Can I have your heart?* But Penny lacks the maturity and experience to be involved with this man, and he should know better.

There must be a balance between two people. One party should not be superior to the other. One should not be at a disadvantage to the other.

Why might people think Penny is being taken advantage of? Because the two are not equal. There is an imbalance in age, experience, knowledge, and wherewithal. Penny does not have those things in equal measure.

A girl writes,

My best friend is 16, and she has recently become infatuated with an older man. He is her dad's best friend, and he is 44.

They have been flirting via text even though he already has a girlfriend. He tells her he fantasizes about her and wants to kiss her. He lives in another city but is visiting soon.

Me and our other best friend have tried to talk her out of it and have even threatened to tell her father, but she won't listen and tells us to mind our own business...

Andrea

We advised Andrea how to protect her friend, even though it might mean losing her friendship.

But more common at this age are crushes. They are the subject of the next chapter.

The main point in this chapter

Young teens lack the maturity to make serious relationship decisions.

Chapter Fourteen

Crushes

You can be in a relationship and be the only one in it. That's one definition of a crush. But the best way to think about a crush is as a dress rehearsal.

A crush is someone an immature person pours their hopes, dreams, and longings onto. When our sexuality comes alive, those feelings will be directed somewhere.

A teenager writes:

I have been obsessed with a male teacher of mine for months. I am a 16-year-old girl, and he's in his late 30s, married, with young children.

We have a nice rapport and are friends in a very appropriate sense. I've been to his place to meet his family a couple of times. He is proper and respectful to me, as a teacher should be. However, I have a huge crush on him. I think about him constantly, and every time we exchange a few words, my heart races.

I hope this obsession will die down, but in the meantime I want to know what to do. I know we can't be more than friends, even though I'd love to kiss him. Should I discuss my feelings with him? I want to talk to him about it, but I don't want him to be uncomfortable.

Darcy

Darcy's crush is not a "we-thing," it's a "me-thing." It's a fantasy in her head. Left alone, it's likely to pass. In addition, some part of her wants to test her powers on an adult male, even though he is not seeking a relationship with her.

I am 16, 17 in a few months. I have fallen head over heels for a man who is 21. He was my camp counselor.

We talk at least once a week, and we talk about everything. Especially deep stuff. I know he genuinely cares about me, but I don't know if he likes me as more than friends. When I confronted him about how I felt, he said, "I'm a counselor and you're a camper, but I do care about you."

Yet his actions say otherwise. He gets nervous around me, and he always puts his arm around me. He held me to make

THE YOUNG WOMAN'S GUIDE TO OLDER MEN

sure I didn't fall. He also said 17 is acceptable for him to date. All my friends noticed his actions too.

I don't know if he's saying he doesn't like me that way because of his job or if he actually doesn't like me that way.

Please help. I don't know what to do, and I love this man.

Gwen

Another young woman writes,

Why can't I just meet the guy that is supposed to be the one and only one for me?

I still hope and believe there is someone for me, and waiting is a process that makes you blissful and extra grateful and loving to that someone when you finally find each other.

Well, about this guy. I guess, when I prayed hard to meet a great guy, I should have been specific with the age range. I should have never grown up, so I don't have to deal with these emotions and stuff.

Your knees shake, you feel weak, you can hear yourself breathe, you can hear the rhythmic beat of your heart, and you make sure he doesn't notice what he's doing to you. I mean, I've been infatuated with other guys, but this is the first time I felt the deeper pain of not being able to express it. Welcome to the world of unrequited love.

I'm in love. It's as simple as that, and it hurts. Love Stinks. Why can't it be simple, honest, and fun?

He likes me and that's the worst part of it. Oh my, we actually like each other. Oh God! I was hoping it was just me and my hormones, but it isn't. He felt it too. I thought it was a crazy crush and would quickly fade away. But I guess it can't be denied—we actually clicked!

What if he's the one? Or is this going to be one of those experiences a person must go through to be tough and to gain wisdom? If it is, then what's the lesson? I didn't choose this, it just happened.

I find myself feeling energetic and positive constantly. But I know under these bewildering circumstances, I have to focus on my head rather than my heart. I'm going to college this fall, and I never planned for this to happen. It's sad, but it's more than I can take.

I've been bombarded with different opinions and looks of disapproval. Everyone's staring and having appalling thoughts about me because of the age factor. The comment that plainly got stuck in my head is, "He's too old for you!"

Inside, I was shocked and confused, but on the outside, I remained calm and in control. The closeness we shared started to come apart. I ignored him. With my young heart being broken apart, I let go.

THE YOUNG WOMAN'S GUIDE TO OLDER MEN

Hopefully, if I hear that song calling me once again, I can be brave enough to fall in love and say to myself, "I and only I can live my life. To hell with all the critics."

Callie

The main point in this chapter

When our sexuality comes alive, those feelings will be directed somewhere. Often, it will be to an inappropriate somewhere.

Chapter Fifteen

The Heart of The Matter

But why is an early, permanent relationship wrong for most women?

I need some advice. Here's my problem.

I met my husband when I was barely 17. I was absolutely taken by him. Or should I say infatuated? He was a lot older, try 17 years older. But I did not find that out until I had fallen in love with him. He lied and told me he was 30, which is still a big age difference.

I found out several months later that he was actually 33. We've been married 13 years and have two beautiful children. I've always struggled with the age difference. I feel like people are always staring at or making judgments about us.

I've always looked young for my age. I am almost 32 and still mistaken for 19. I've recently started to have a problem with our relationship. I've grown up a lot over the years and look back a lot. I dwell on the fact that I was sooooooo young when our relationship started.

A lot of times I feel the only reason I am here is because I love my children so much. I don't want them to grow up in a divorced family. My husband is the kindest, sweetest guy. Any woman would be lucky to have him, but I have to ask myself what was he thinking when he decided to pursue this relationship?

I look at people 16 years younger than me as kids, and I'm not even the age he was when he met me. I'm bothered by the whole thing.

Sylvia

Sylvia's letter is about lost youth and lost possibilities. At 31, with two children, she could still pass for 19. It seems almost possible to regain the freedom of a 19-year-old, but she knows she can't.

Now she is cracking under the weight of her life, knowing what she knows today. At 17, she couldn't look far enough into the future to see the day when her husband would be 48 and she'd be 31, wishing she was 19 again. All she can do now is wonder why her husband would get involved with a child.

THE YOUNG WOMAN'S GUIDE TO OLDER MEN

Typically, it falls on the older party to say no, and, ultimately, if it's genuine love, it will hang on and it will wait. The older party should understand this. They should not be the one acting without forethought. But if their interest in you is because you're a child, they won't wait.

The following letter, though written by a young man, illustrates what Sylvia's life might have been.

I met a girl when I was a senior in college, and she was a freshman. We dated all throughout her college years. Though it was a long-distance relationship, we made it work.

She graduated and took a job three hours away from me, and we began to plan for me to move up and live with her. I asked her to marry me and she said yes.

A week later, she calls and tells me she can't and it's over. Her reason is that she can't get over how emotionally distant I am. I admit I am reserved, but I never hurt her intentionally, and she admits our relationship was good.

I don't get what happened. When we last saw each other, she told me she loves me so much and will miss me, and if she could fix the problem she would, but she doesn't see a way. A lot of people tell me she got scared and confused with her life change—a new place, a job, and being on her own for the first time.

WAYNE & TAMARA MITCHELL

She still wants to talk and tell me what's going on in her life. I don't know. Is it over or is she still making her decision? I don't want to wait around and talk to her because then I'll never be able to let go. At the same time, if there's a chance for this to work out, I don't want to give up.

Quinn

Our answer:

Quinn, it's a bit of this. When I was a child, I spoke as a child, I understood as a child, I thought as a child. Now I have put away my childish things. Then I saw through a mirror darkly. Now I'm a newly minted adult with a college degree and a job. I've grown up.

When you two started dating, you were a senior in college, and she was a freshman. In her mind, you were more mature and sophisticated than the boys she knew.

Now she's been a senior herself. She's seen lots of guys: mature guys, sophisticated guys, guys who have done stuff. What you have done, she has done. She's no longer the little girl fresh out of high school looking up to a college senior.

Your emotional distance might mean she can't tell if you love her more than you love potato salad. Maybe there's something to that, but probably not. You must remember, when someone breaks up with you, they have to say something. The reason often has little to do with you and more to do with them.

THE YOUNG WOMAN'S GUIDE TO OLDER MEN

She's got options she didn't have four years ago, and she knows it. Your relationship worked for a time, and in dating, that's often what it is. It worked for a time. Her ease and coolness in becoming your "friend" shows she has already left your relationship behind.

Letting her talk to you as if she hadn't just broken off your engagement isn't good for you. You already know you need separation so you can move on.

Sometimes we need to count our blessings for an event that did not occur. In figuring out where she is in life, she helped you understand where you are in life.

Wayne & Tamara

Quinn's girlfriend is a different person now.

When a young person has a job, their own apartment, and some money, the standard of what is acceptable will differ from when they lacked the necessities for independence. Who a teenager is at 18 will differ from who they are at 24, with or without a college degree. At 24, they will be attracted to different people, and different people will be attracted to them.

The next writer presents her dilemma clearly.

I met my boyfriend when I was 18 and he was 38. I'm 20, he's now 40, and I am about to graduate from college. I feel like I've been thrown into a world that isn't right for my age. (But my age isn't exactly right for me either. I typically have friends in their mid- to late-20s).

I'm done with the whole college thing really, but I want to enjoy my 20s and do physical activities and go enjoy life. And with someone older, "Do I want someone who's already had so much more experience than me? Do I want to grow up with this man?"

What's been on my mind is shouldn't these be my constructive years, the years when I meet people, make connections, and get to know myself and what I want? I see a future with him, but right now I feel like I'm missing my youth in a way, and I don't want to be taking care of an elderly person my entire life.

Bottom line is I don't want to have regrets in the future. I don't want to be lonely, miserable, or stuck in a marriage, but I don't want to lose the one person I care about.

Ginger

The following writer is in a different situation.

My name is Alexandria, and I am a 29-year-old woman who works for a home care agency. Recently, I was working

THE YOUNG WOMAN'S GUIDE TO OLDER MEN

in a home with a 97-year-old woman who was living with her 62-year-old son. Well, yesterday, he invited me to dinner at his home and we went to the movies afterwards.

At no point did he act inappropriately toward me, nor I to him. Yet I could sense a definite attraction to me, and I cannot deny that I have similar feelings for him.

I am no longer working for Tom, as his mother died almost two weeks ago. (The agency expressly forbids contact with clients outside work hours.) Since I am no longer working there, I felt free to accept his invitation.

We had a great time last night. At the end of the evening, I gave him an innocent hug. It felt wonderful. When I came home this afternoon, there was a message on my email from Tom. He said, "I just want you to know that you are ruining my concentration."

Tom is older than my own father. I barely slept last night. My palms are so sweaty I can barely type. I don't want to lose him or his friendship. How do I proceed? I am a wreck.

Alexandria

Alexandria has enough experience of life to make her own decisions. If she wants to date Tom and see where it leads, she is free to make that choice.

The main point in this chapter

Our perspective changes as we age.

Chapter Sixteen

The Ideal Age Difference

Some people claim there is an ideal age difference in relationships.

A dating rule from the 1800s says, when a woman marries, she should be half the age of her husband, plus 7 years.[1] That rule dates from a time when clerks measured a yard of cloth from the tip of their nose to the tip of their fingers. Though the rule is outdated, it had one virtue. It wagged a disapproving finger at old men who wanted to marry young girls.

Today, some people have modernized the Rule of 7s as a dating rule for both sexes.[2] Either gender can be half the age of the other person, plus 7 years. However, that is not the way most women date.

A third rule calculates the oldest person you should date.[3] Take your age, subtract 7, and multiply by 2. At 20, don't date anyone over 26; at 30, don't date anyone over 46, et cetera.

A final rule suggests dating only those within a fifth of your age.[4]

So which rule is right? None of them.

It is impossible to pick a "right" age spread or to say if there should be a spread at all. Not every 18-year-old goes to college; not every 19-year-old lives with their parents. Our life experiences are not the same.

There is no "ideal" age difference because age is more than years. We can be socially a certain age, chronologically a certain age, medically a certain age, intellectually a certain age, and emotionally a certain age.

And the various rules say nothing about love.

In 2014, newspapers reported a study that predicted the likelihood of divorce based on the age gap of the couple. Curious, we looked up the study. What we found was the study wasn't about age gap at all.[5]

Instead, a data scientist took numbers from the study and drew his own conclusions—until the authors of the original study pointed out why his conclusions were not valid.[6] Unfortunately, you can still find internet articles repeating this flawed analysis.

Other studies make different claims. A British study found "...despite any popular belief to the contrary, there does not appear to be any strong association between marital age difference and probability of divorce."[7] A Dutch study claimed divorce was more likely if the man was more than five years older.[8] A Canadian study claimed divorce rates were lowest when the husband was 2 to 10 years older.[9] And an American study argued, "woman-older partners reported the highest levels of romantic satisfaction and commitment."[10]

The lesson we draw is this. Be cautious reading age gap studies. At most, they are gross assessments of a population, not guides for individuals.

The main point in this chapter

None of the age gap rules, and none of the age gap studies, contain the secret relationship sauce.

CHAPTER SEVENTEEN

Voices of Success

By now, you might wonder if age gap relationships ever work. The answer is yes.

I'm currently in the classic older man and younger woman relationship. I'm 50, Nancy is 30, and we are both divorced. I was not looking for anyone when Nancy came into my life. She is beautiful and sweet, and I absolutely adore her.

I could think of a million reasons why it doesn't make sense to have a relationship with a younger woman. But she doesn't feel that way at all. So why am I writing? At this juncture in my life, I simply can't see this relationship in the long term.

I told Nancy not to waste time with someone like me; I have far less life to live than she does. She insists I have plenty of time left, though I cannot see where this could possibly go and be good for both of us. Am I simply sounding like some insecure, middle-aged idiot, or should I enjoy what we have and see where it leads?

Simon

In our newspaper column, we told Simon:

If you know something in your own heart that prevents this, or if there is an issue you haven't resolved, such as having children, that's one thing. But if it's simply the idea of the years, the years don't matter.

To suggest the difference in age is the problem implies being close in age would guarantee success. But that isn't true. Many couples in the United States divorce and most of them are close in age.

It is love that is the center of everything, not the number of years since your birth. It is love that creates alignment and balance between two people. What matters is that you love each other and belong together.

Being an insecure, middle-aged idiot is no fun, so we suggest you enjoy what you have and see where it leads.

Wayne & Tamara

A reader responded:

THE YOUNG WOMAN'S GUIDE TO OLDER MEN

Unless you have a May–December marriage, you have no right to tell a 50-year-old and a 30-year-old to go ahead and get married.

There is nothing good about these marriages. Women caught in this situation put up a front because they don't want to admit they were bilked into a painful situation.

True, we could argue this until Jesus returns. Joseph was evidently much older than Mary; however, where was he at the time of the crucifixion? Dead, or not there anyway. What does that tell us? Someone else had to take his place: namely the Apostle John.

In social groups, there is no place for May–December marriages. The women in the older groups do not accept the younger woman and the younger groups don't accept the older man.

I speak with authority. I spent 41 years of torture with a man 20 years older than I was because I did not believe in divorce. Older men have their mindset established and the wife can either follow or be miserable.

I have yet to see a happy May–December marriage. Sometimes you will hear kids say, "My parents, my aunt and uncle and so on, were happy, although there was a big age difference." Just get the women off by themselves and see what they have to say. It is all a big front.

I chose to be happy in spite of the old goat. I believe, like Abe Lincoln, "We are all about as happy as we choose to be." However, why not save the pain of May–December marriages before they happen?

Luella

Our reply...

Luella, we believe the problem in your marriage was your husband's personality, not the difference in your ages. We have known many happy couples with a significant age difference. It is less common, but in some of these couples, the wife was the older partner.

The following is a letter we received from Spain in response to the age difference column you wrote about.

"Simon, I am sure you are going to get a rush of letters telling you not to be foolish. In our case (Harry 82 and Patricia 60), we met when I was 57 and Pat was 35. At first, I did not want her to know my age, thinking the same sorts of things as you do. My daughter informed me she already knew my age.

"After that small fear was over, we married and spent the last 25 years having a wonderful, loving relationship, which we hope will carry on forever and ever. So take our advice and give Nancy the chance to make you both happy for the next 25 years and beyond. Harry."

Another reader added to the conversation...

I ran across your advice about big age differences in marriages, and I have to say Luella is projecting from her own marriage. I have been married for over 32 years to a man 29 years my senior, since I was 19.

If it had been an arranged marriage, I would have been unhappy and thought I was missing something, but it was my own choice. I had been with enough guys my own age that I knew enough to value him, even though I was young.

I thank God for him every day, and see some of my agemates in bitter, unhappy marriages with guys their own age. It isn't for everyone, and there is no question that he is likely to go before me, but in the meantime, I've had 32 years of happiness with the most interesting, loving person I know.

I had cancer a couple of years ago, and he had to face the prospect of life without me. Fortunately, I recovered, but I am grateful to take my happiness where I can find it and let the future take care of itself.

Elsa

Maturity is hard to measure, which is why age is only one consideration. Some young people are wise beyond their years, and some old people never grow up.

As a final note, though the common term is "a May-December relationship," "May-September" more accurately describes most of these relationships.

The main point in this chapter

Neither age difference, nor closeness in age, can predict happiness in a relationship.

Chapter Eighteen

Should I Go Forward?

The toughest thing for many people is to acknowledge exactly what their relationship is. You can't lie to yourself. You can't play Pinocchio about what your relationship is and expect success.

My boyfriend and I have been together two and a half years and have lived together six months. I moved into his house. We began talking about marriage after a year, and I have been assuming nothing but marriage ever since.

He is 12 years older than me and financially stable. He has a stable personality and life, both of which appealed to me from the beginning.

I was a bit of a rebel before I met him. I always dated "bad boys" and was extremely attracted to them, but things were always unstable. My boyfriend now is clean-cut and not a bad boy at all.

I did not have a problem with any of this before. All this stability and thoughts of marriage were exciting, but now I find myself at a crossroads. I am not attracted to him and have a hard time "turning on." I feel like we are roommates and buddies, more than two people thinking about marriage.

I get irritated easily with his advances toward me and find myself disgusted by how sensitive he can be. But I don't know if I would be a fool to leave.

He's a great man, and I love his family and friends. We have a dog together and that makes it complicated as well. Should I marry him for comfort and security, or go find a "bad boy" who turns me on?

Emily

Emily is not in love with her boyfriend. If she marries him, she may get security, but it's unrealistic to expect love to follow. If she marries a "bad boy," she should expect a volatile life.

The way our needs work is simple. When one need is satisfied, other needs emerge. When you partner with someone to fill a lesser need, like security, you should not believe it will transform into love. More likely, you will find that need still unfulfilled.

THE YOUNG WOMAN'S GUIDE TO OLDER MEN

When money and security are the deciding factors, the couple can be blown apart by what money cannot purchase...

I am attracted to my own stepson.

My husband (48) and I (29) have been married for five years now. One of his sons had been living with us for the past two and a half years. He is 23. My stepson and I had a tough time accepting each other, but by the time we did, seven or eight months ago, the unexpected results emerged.

We love each other with true passion, and the feeling does not seem to go anywhere, no matter how hard we try. And boy, we did try hard.

Naturally, this has been a platonic love, for we allowed only minimal physical contact between us. But the attraction is so incredibly powerful, on both sides, that it is almost unbelievable. Sometimes we look at each other and you can see the sparks flying and feel the earth moving.

Many people never come across such attraction in their entire lifetime, but for us it has been going on constantly for at least seven months. Every time we look at each other, every time we stand close to each other, every time we speak on the phone, we can feel the incredible passion. We simply complete each other.

Obviously, not having physical love when absolutely everything else is there is now causing problems. How long can a person stand intense passion without physical closeness?

Being around each other now feels like a never-ending emotional crisis. The other day, he offered to rent an apartment and asked me to leave his father and move in with him. He has been talking about having children and a family. I began crying because I can't feel an ounce of strength in me anymore. I don't know what to do.

His father gives me material safety, but his son gives me everything else a woman could wish for: love, caring, respect, understanding, intensity, dedication, patience. The packaging is extremely attractive too; he is truly good-looking, strong in mind and body, and extremely intelligent. If only heart mattered, I would pack right now and leave with him. I wouldn't think twice.

But I must think about the age difference and how he and I would feel about each other 10 years down the road. He'll be 33 and I'll be 39 and not as attractive then as now. And I must think about his and his father's relationship, as well as the other two brothers.

I love him, and I don't want him to have regrets or feel pain in the future, if his relationship with his dad and siblings goes straight down the drain because of his decisions today.

How about having both men? Can it be done? Can he and I be happy like that? Can his father and I be happy like that?

And can he and his father still have a good relationship if his son and I are physically close to each other?

Christine

Lucia has a different problem…

I am a 23-year-old female and currently in a relationship with a man 14 years my senior. I've been enjoying my relationship with him, and we wanted to get married. I'm scared of what my family will say about this relationship, because I have managed to keep it from my father. I know he won't approve, and his approval means a lot to me.

I recently met this guy who is just wonderful and my age. Though I hate to admit it, I've developed deep feelings, but I don't know whether to call it love. I told him about my boyfriend, but not about the age difference.

He is convinced that he and I were meant for each other, and I believe we could build something strong. I hate cheating on my boyfriend. I know I have to make a decision, but I can't seem to decide.

If I break up with my boyfriend, he will be devastated, but I don't want to stay with him because I'm scared of hurting him. I do love him, and I don't want to leave him because I'm scared of disappointing my father. On the other hand, I enjoy the other guy's company, but I'm not sure who I love.

Lucia

Lucia is in the classic "torn between two lovers" dilemma. That usually means neither man is right, at least not now. Love decides. Love is not comparison shopping.

Lucia is right in thinking she shouldn't stay with the older man because she fears hurting him. It always amazes us how many people end up married to someone because they didn't have the courage to break up with them.

Another woman writes:

My name is Meredith. I am 27 and my boss is 46. I was wondering if it is inappropriate for me to have a personal or friendship relationship with him.

He is literally ALMOST ALWAYS THERE for me. ALWAYS tells me he is there if I need him. He emails me electronic cards: GET-WELL CARDS, CHRISTMAS, and NEW YEARS. We EMAIL each other AND text each other.

I've been out with him and some others for a goodbye party for his secretary. I ENJOY HIS COMPANY VERY, VERY MUCH. He is a bit of a womanizer though. He is currently living with one woman, left his first wife, AND has some weird relationship with another girl, 36.

THE YOUNG WOMAN'S GUIDE TO OLDER MEN

My parents don't approve of our relationship because of his other relationships, AND because of what it might do to my job, if something wrong happens.

I HAVE ALWAYS AND STILL CONTINUE TO FEEL COMPLETELY COMFORTABLE AND RELAXED WITH HIM. I DO NOT FEEL THREATENED OR UNCOMFORTABLE BEING ALONE WITH HIM AT ALL.

I've been ALONE with him in his office SEVERAL times, and he has NEVER done anything for me to feel uneasy around him.

DO YOU THINK I CAN KEEP THE RELATIONSHIP OR DO YOU FEEL IT'S WRONG?

Meredith

We told Meredith:

Whether it's learning a language, running a business, or starting a relationship, pattern recognition is critical. The mail carrier comes each day at one, and we learn when to have the outgoing mail ready. We hear the wail of a siren, and we pull over to let a fire engine pass.

One of the most important functions of pattern recognition is to protect us, but it can't do that if we ignore the pattern or refuse to see it. Your boss is a womanizer. He is involved with several women and grooming at least one more, you, to join the stable. His pattern of behavior is repeated every day, from the factory floor to the White House.

Perhaps you haven't been in this situation before, so you don't know what the end result is. Perhaps you don't realize each woman entering a relationship with him thought she would be the last. The truth is, his pattern doesn't fit what you are looking for, but as long as women line up to be with him, he can only conclude what he is doing works—for him.

Don't give him credit for saying he is there if you need him. That statement will likely never be put to a real test. Making women feel comfortable with him is his method of operation. Can you see his pattern, or will you learn an awfully hard lesson, the kind of lesson that makes you mistrust other men—good, honest men?

Hi, I am constantly sitting here fighting with myself about what to do. I am 21 and I think I am in love with a man 37. Actually, I KNOW I'm in love with him. I have known him for a year now. We are not in a relationship, but I see him almost every week.

Here's the dilemma: we only talk on the phone when we are going to meet up, or sometimes he texts me, recommending a movie to watch (he's a big movie buff). I thought I was maybe a booty call for a while, from reading other sites and the bullet points they make. Some pertain to me, but I can't tell if I'm in denial when I try to put a good spin on it.

I met his family and most of his friends.

THE YOUNG WOMAN'S GUIDE TO OLDER MEN

He took me to a wedding as his date. I went on a camping trip with him and his friends before, BUT we also only see each other mostly on weekends and don't talk unless we are seeing each other.

Almost every time I see him, we have sex, but I also sleep over. A lot of times I meet up with him late at night, but that's usually my fault because he asks me out earlier and I am already busy but can meet him later.

(I am sorry that I'm all over the place with this letter. I have all these thoughts racing through my mind!)

What I guess I am getting to is, do you think it's worth pursuing this in hopes it will turn into something more, even though there are a lot of obstacles? He is busy having a life that a regular 37-year-old would have, and I am doing things that a 21-year-old usually does. I am SO VERY confused where I stand with him, and I don't know how to ask him.

Here's a tough one: sometimes we go places, like when he took me to the wedding as his date. Some people he knows would come up and say, "Hey, why don't I set you up with another guy, someone more your age?" Then they would ask his opinion, and my guy would respond, saying, "Do what you want to do," or, "It doesn't matter to me."

But that is the only time he says it like that. He acknowledges that I'm young, but in a bad way, when I am with him. I don't know if this thing we have has an opportunity to turn into more because I am head over heels for him and don't want to be hurt.

Jane

A man who loves a woman would never say, "Do what you want to do. It doesn't matter to me." Jane's boyfriend sees her as an object of convenience.

When you marry someone, you marry their character and their marital history.

Hello Wayne and Tamara,

I've been engaged almost two years and my wedding date is approaching in July, but I'm unsure. My parents think he has too much baggage. We've been together a little over three years and he's 14 years older than me. While we have so much in common, we've also had a series of events that dampened our relationship.

We both have two children, close in age, who get along well. I have never been married, and upon meeting, he said he wasn't married. Well, my dad is an ex-cop, and in his free time three or four months into the relationship, he looked up my (at the time) boyfriend and a search showed there was a woman with his last name related to or living with him.

THE YOUNG WOMAN'S GUIDE TO OLDER MEN

When I confronted him, he came clean and said he was married but separated. I was devastated. I was in total shock. My mother didn't think it was the end of the world since he was separated. My instincts said let him go, but I listened to my mom's advice and continued to date him.

He filed for a divorce, but that opened the floodgates to his psycho ex-wife, who would rather not have him be a part of his kids' lives. She purposely caused him financial ruin before the divorce was final.

She attacked me at his son's football game. She lied to get a protection order, saying she feared for her and the kids' lives, but it was to keep him away. She's constantly taking him to court for money and to reduce his already limited time with the kids. It is all out of spite, but has clearly taken a toll on the children.

From there, other lies were revealed that didn't have anything to do with me or our time together, but it's made it hard to trust him. He has worked hard to be transparent with me. He's loving, he's kind, he's patient through all of my unsureness. But I haven't reached a place where I'm sure I want to marry him and all that he comes with.

Time is ticking and a lot of money is on the line if I don't decide soon.

Emma

We told Emma the basis of her interest in him was founded on a lie, and there have been more lies since. Add in the problems with his ex, and this is a disaster in the making.

We knew a large, beefy man, an executive with a railroad, married 35 years. He was plainspoken to the point of being blunt. But once, on a weekend at a park, when asked where his wife was, he replied, "She's gamboling on the green."

Gambol is a rare word, which means to prance like a deer or to skip about. He spoke that way about his rather plump, middle-aged wife without a hint of irony. He spoke like a poet, as if trying to describe a color the rest of us can't see.

That's what you are looking for.

But in many relationships, it's as if the person went shopping for a dog and brought home a cat. Then they complain their cat can't bark.

The main point in this chapter

If you play Pinocchio about what your relationship is, you won't end up with a long nose. You'll end up with the wrong man.

The second most important point

Your love has value. When you discount the value of your love, you are apt to throw it away.

Chapter Nineteen

How to Tell Family and Friends

I have recently begun a May–December relationship with the most wonderful man I ever met. I am 22, and he is 40. We had been good friends for over a year before we decided that our feelings were turning a different direction.

Everything seems perfect. We have the same taste in technology, food, music, and activities. We also seem to balance each other: he is bold, talkative, and energetic, while I am contemplative, shy, and relaxed. Our biggest worry is our families.

He has not dated in nearly 12 years (I am divorced), and while his daughter said (before we got together) she would be happy for him to start dating, she's not giving many clues on how she feels now that he is.

Not only that, how to tell her about our age difference! The daughter's mother and he are on good terms, but not able to have a good, working, romantic relationship.

I have no need or intention of trying to be the "new mom." Our mutual friends are fine with "us," but we wonder how to tell our families, specifically his daughter, that we are real.

Grace

A young woman in the identical situation writes:

... Now it has come to the point that I am willing to tell all. I hate hiding and it affects me every day. But with that comes hurting the family and disappointing them. I try to equalize my options, weigh it out, and I only wish that I would not be judged. At the same time, I can't blame my family because most of society thinks the same.

This relationship is extremely important to me, and I don't want it to crash and burn. I appreciate him and our relationship so much that I would be willing to take anything I could get, if it must be. I just don't want to hide anymore; it doesn't feel right hiding something so precious and lovely in my life...

THE YOUNG WOMAN'S GUIDE TO OLDER MEN

This chapter is not about whether either of those relationships should move forward. It is about how to reveal your age gap relationship to others.

Two researchers, Alan Manning and Nicole Amare, found that when the news you carry involves a grave physical threat, such as you have cancer, people want the truth immediately.[1]

But things are different in social situations. While people value directness, they need a word of warning first. As Manning says, "...all you need is a 'we need to talk' buffer—just a couple of seconds for the other person to process that bad news is coming."[2] That buffer allows the other party to shift their emotional state.

Older research suggested warming up to the topic and dragging out the message. But Manning and Amare believe that makes it easier on the messenger, but not on the recipient.

We can't find any studies on how to reveal an age difference relationship. However, many studies tell doctors the best way to impart information, and many other studies tell managers how to handle a hard conversation.[3] We've picked the seven best points from this research.

The 7 Steps:

    1. Remember why this conversation is necessary. It is

the first step to living in the world with someone in a normal way and without apology.

2. Rehearse, but don't over rehearse what you will say.

3. Don't approach this as a win-or-lose issue. (You need not win the other person over.)

4. Be prepared for any reaction.

5. Provide a buffer at the beginning. (Say something like, "We need to talk.")

6. Let the other party have their say.

7. Leave if there are threats or abuse.

The meeting will go as it goes, and at this stage, you don't have to agree to anything.

A word of caution: Never, ever go to a face-to-face meeting if you believe there is even a remote chance of violence, coercion, or kidnapping.

Let us emphasize why the first step is necessary. You desire to live in the world normally and without apology.

A man writes:

THE YOUNG WOMAN'S GUIDE TO OLDER MEN

I find myself in an extremely uncomfortable situation. I am single, never married and in my early 40s. I have some friends, a married couple, who I spend a decent amount of time around. They aren't my closest friends, but after my four or five best friends, they are probably on the next rung of the friendship ladder.

Three years ago, their (at the time) 19-year-old and exceedingly attractive daughter made a somewhat awkward but ultimately successful pass at me. We soon began a relationship, completely under the radar of our family, friends, and social circle.

It started off as purely sexual but evolved into what we both know is true love, despite the almost 20-year age difference. We are nuts about each other and want to spend more time together, but if we do, we risk being found out.

We both detest the thought of having to reveal our relationship to her parents. They are pretty traditional, and I can see them viewing this as some kind of betrayal on my part. They will most assuredly think it highly inappropriate, at the least. Opening up publicly is going to be possibly the most difficult thing I've ever had to do.

We both agree we can't keep this circumstance going as is indefinitely. We've considered ending things but can't stand the thought of never again being together. Plus, we would still be in the unfortunate position of having to see each other.

I am at wits' end about how to approach this. I love her very much, but I have a sense of dread about how it might affect both of our relationships with her folks, if we reveal what has been going on.

Pete

Pete has two problems. For one, he has played the wolf in sheep's clothing. That taints how he views himself and how others will view him.

But the broader point is that neither Pete nor his girlfriend can know how they actually feel. They have been living in a bubble of secrecy and lies. They have not had a normal relationship: out, visible, interacting with family and friends. There is no way for them to tell what their relationship is.

The main point in this chapter

There is a best way to deliver "unwelcome news."

The second most important point

You won't know how you feel about a man until you are with him openly.

Chapter Twenty

Another Word About Telling

Sometimes we think others believe as we believe. Often they don't. As Alan Manning says, "People's belief systems are where they are most touchy. So any message that affects their belief system, their ego identity, that's what you've got to buffer."[1]

Three researchers at the Harvard Negotiation Project say nearly the same thing. They compare delivering a tough message to lobbing a hand grenade. But, they warn, if you say nothing, it solves nothing. That would be like pulling the pin on the grenade and holding on to it.[2]

In *Difficult Conversations*, the three researchers—Douglas Stone, Bruce Patton, and Sheila Heen—say hard discussions can make you feel an "identity quake."[3] The mere thought of the conversation can make you doubt yourself and feel you are incompetent or a bad person. But those feelings may have little basis in fact.

We suggest doing one thing before you tell: do your best to separate what is important to you from what is *most important* to you.

That often means determining where your parents, or others, fit in your life. Here are two typical situations:

I am 18 years old and in a relationship with a guy 20 years older. While I was a teenager, I never hung out with people my age but always with people who were in their 20s and 30s. I even graduated high school one year early, and now have one year left before I get my degree.

My family is against our relationship because of the age difference. I don't want to disappoint them, but I feel that if I am happy, why can't I stay happy? My parents want me to be with someone my age. I can't help the fact that I like older men. I have tried to date younger ones, but I don't get along with them and always have a horrible time.

THE YOUNG WOMAN'S GUIDE TO OLDER MEN

In my relationship, all of our goals are the same, and when we go out, we have so much fun just being around each other. He acts and looks ten years younger than he is, anyway.

Many times I feel pressured to give it all up because of what my parents say, but then I think, if I were to see him later in life married to someone else, I would regret it. I'm not scared of making a mistake, but I don't want to disappoint my parents.

Should I be worried about what they think? I want to marry him and start a family.

Taylor

Underlying Taylor's letter is the fear of missing out. She doesn't want to be like this woman...

I am a 76-year-old woman who has never been in love. I have one shining memory of what might have grown into love from 50 years ago, but I was young and stupid and treated the connection callously, and the young man went away. But I remember vividly the feeling. It was wonderful.

Another woman writes:

WAYNE & TAMARA MITCHELL

My boyfriend and I have an 11-year age gap. He is 38, I am 27. My parents have a problem with this. They are in their 40s and had me when they were teenagers. I was a surprise.

My dad told me he wouldn't accept it if we ever got married. We aren't at that point yet, but I feel I am shortchanging my boyfriend because I hold back due to my parents.

We were hesitant to date because of our age difference, then we realized it doesn't matter. We have a lot in common and our maturity level is compatible. How do I get my parents to open up to him and give him a chance?

Wendi

We told Wendi:

You're an adult woman, not your parents' 17-year-old daughter. If you had followed your parents' example, you would already be married with a 10-year-old child.

Your parents got to decide where you went to school, what clothes you wore, and what time you had to come home. Those times are over. You're an adult, so act like it.

What is the major criterion for marriage? Love, or being the same age? If you love him, move forward. If you don't, stop dating him.

If your mom and dad did a good job parenting, they should trust you to make an adult decision. If they didn't do a good job parenting, why should you listen to them now?

THE YOUNG WOMAN'S GUIDE TO OLDER MEN

Sometimes telling results in emotional blackmail or extortion...

Ours is a magical relationship. I am a 27-year-old, and he is 55. We have been together for more than a year.

I met him when I went abroad for a work assignment. He is simply marvelous, intelligent, jovial, and very, very understanding. He thinks I am wise beyond my years because I am caring in advising on matters of health, finance, and career.

Adding to the age differences are our cultural differences. I am an Asian, born and brought up to think about others before I think about myself, and also to consider how my actions impact my family. He is an American, radical in his thoughts, a man who does not believe in societal crap.

He says people who love each other should never go to sleep angry with each other. We stay 8,000 miles away and are able to carry out our relationship and make it stronger and more understanding.

Recently, I told my parents about us, and of course they did not agree. They think I have no future with him. They also said, if I go ahead with him, they will go away in exile and never let me know their whereabouts.

They will also call my siblings back home. They will not let them study further or work in another city.

Now I am in such a dilemma. I want him who I love and want to spend the rest of my life with, as well as my parents, who gave me birth and made sure I grew up to be an intelligent and sensitive human being. I'm writing because I am unable to make any decision.

Riya

The main point in this chapter

Before you tell, you may need to separate what is important in your life from what is *most important* in your life.

The second most important point

There is an alternative to the difficult conversation. If you are a mature adult, you don't need permission.

Chapter Twenty-One

Stages of Life

Who we are has been constructed in a forward direction since the moment of our birth. The longer we've been alive, the more set that construction is. Our foundations were set in how, when, and where we were raised. Our foundations were set by what we learned, did, and saw.

When you're in an age gap relationship, you may want to be with someone who has lived a different way and done different things. It can be fun; it can excite; it can be an adventure. But sometimes, only for a time.

Typically, the people in our group, our peers, are much like us. They are similar, not opposite. But with an age difference, there can be daily assaults on the uncommon elements in the relationship.

We change as we age, and as we age, we come into the characteristics of another stage in life. In a gap relationship, both parties are not in the same stage. They may even be two stages apart. A 20-something is not like a 40-something. A younger person may want to seem older, or an older person may want to seem younger, but neither may be in their natural state.

In the thrall of romance, either of them might think, *I could be this person,* or, *I could be more like that. I could be what I aspire to be.* But when people act out of character, it is a temporary, not a lasting, change. People revert to the mean—their average, normal, typical behavior.

In the same way, we can't judge anyone by how they act over the holidays. It's who they are on an ordinary day that counts.

The following letter illustrates the issue with different life stages:

I am currently in a "May–December" relationship. I am 19 and he is 42. We knew each other from work for about a year and a half before we started dating and now have been together for over a year. We love each other very much and plan to stay together. It was difficult at first, after we told people about us, except for my best friend, who I told right away. She was very supportive and happy for us.

THE YOUNG WOMAN'S GUIDE TO OLDER MEN

Everywhere we went, and go now, we get dirty looks, especially from older women. Usually the men cheer my boyfriend on, which I don't mind. But the women, they don't hide their disgust.

I've gotten much more comfortable in public with him, but the first few months were a little rocky. He was always worried I was too young, but our problems have strengthened our relationship because our love for each other overcame the jealousy or the fear or the uncertainty.

Anyway, even though I don't hide our relationship in public anymore, the looks and comments still bother me. The reasons don't matter; whether they think I'm using him, or he's using me, or I have father issues, or he's a dirty old man. It's strange; people are accepting interracial couples and gay and lesbian couples, but the age difference is taboo.

His whole family is extremely supportive and has welcomed me with open arms, and most of my friends have too. I know I'll never find anyone like him again, and I wish other people in our situation the best.

All the excuses people give me that we shouldn't be together (it's unhealthy, there are too many problems for it to be worth it) are just various stereotypes manifesting themselves into, "It's because I care about you."

I don't know what else to say. I just wanted to add to the conversation.

Harper

For the younger partner, there is a vast difference between an imagined future with a man and the reality of living with him, just as there is a difference between knowing you must get up throughout the night with a newborn, and doing it.

That's what maturity entails—a sense of what things will be like.

Things work in reverse in the next letter. The reality of being with a younger woman doesn't match this man's fantasy...

I'm 23; my boyfriend is 45. He was married before and has three children. At first, he claimed he wanted to marry me and spend the rest of his life with me. I grew to love him a lot, so I decided to give him a chance to prove his love.

Well, lately I find every time I call he's either busy or about to do something else. I know he's busy. He holds a demanding job. But he had just stated he would make time for me. Also, he doesn't talk to me at all. I mean, he won't sit down and talk.

At first he would make love to me so passionately it was unbelievable. Now I have to ask and it's routine, as if he does it "just because." He stopped saying, "I love you." He used to make sure I had everything to make me comfortable. Now that is no more.

THE YOUNG WOMAN'S GUIDE TO OLDER MEN

He used to allow me to answer his phone. Now, when I'm there, he lets the phone ring. If I ask to answer, he says, "Let them call back." I think he is seeing someone else.

I'm confused, and this hurts me. I don't want to lose him. I'm a fun type, and he isn't complying. I know he's a nice person, but what is the problem?

Lise

Compromise is not the answer to problems arising from different stages of life. Compromise means someone will lose what they want from life.

Though some people act like everything can be compromised, children are the first issue that proves that is false.

I've been married for four years to a wonderful, fun-loving man with whom I share many things—including a sincere friendship, a passionate sex life, and a love of being creative. I couldn't be happier in my marriage with him.

The only problem is our differing views on having children. He has a grown child from a previous marriage. I have no children. He is 10 years older than me. I would like to try to start a family and he is reluctant. He thinks he is too old to start this again; he knows (he says) the enormous work it takes, and he loves the freedom we have to do what we want when we want.

I believe, though, that his feelings have much more to do with his first marriage. His first wife made motherhood her only focus after their child was born, and my husband felt like the "seed donor." Their marriage deteriorated so badly that, even years after the divorce, his first wife refuses to speak with him.

I knew about his mixed feelings when we married. I hoped time would change this. Though I have absolutely no desire to let this turn into something that breaks us up or causes irreparable damage, I am now occasionally experiencing feelings of resentment. (How can he do this to ME? I've always wanted children, and HE'S denying me my chance, et cetera.) I don't believe, however, that this should be only MY choice—it is ours.

But I'm in a quandary and feel like time is running out as I approach 35.

On top of all this, we are both fond of children and frequently spend time with friends who have children. We're always asked if we plan to have children and when—and people comment about our obvious love for children.

So... help!

Stephanie

THE YOUNG WOMAN'S GUIDE TO OLDER MEN

Stephanie, in our mind's eye, we picture you and your groom standing at the altar at your wedding. The minister solemnly intones the line, "If anyone knows why this couple cannot be joined in holy matrimony, let them speak now or forever hold their peace." Unlike some old movies, no one comes forward.

But there is one person who knows a reason the wedding shouldn't occur. She holds her peace...that person is you.

Your husband was upfront with you. He had three reasons he didn't want to start a family: he felt he was too old, he felt it was too demanding, and he didn't want to give up his freedom. His reasons were based on experience.

And you? You have every right to want children. But if you felt this way before the wedding, either you concealed a material fact in order to get married, or you decided you were going to make this decision regardless of how he felt. It is the ancient complaint of men...after the wedding, she changed.

There is no room for compromise on this one. You can't have half a child and we can't give you the words to make him come around to your point of view. Children need to come into this world when they are wanted by both parents with all their hearts. They should come from joy and unity. When they come from resentment, conflict, or a terrible compromise, it is an injustice to everyone.

You did yourself a disservice to marry a man who doesn't want children. Nobody is going to be happy with this, and he may end up losing two wives over the same issue.

You can't continue in the same manner, refusing to admit it isn't what he has done to you, but the position you put yourself in. Put everything on the table. You need to be totally honest with your husband and let whatever happens come from honesty—not from secret agendas, "accidental pregnancy," or hidden resentments.

Wayne & Tamara

The main point in this chapter

You must decide whether the differing stages of life make your relationship impossible.

Chapter Twenty-Two

Three Principles

In the beginning of a relationship, there are things you can't see or won't see. When you are in newness and infatuation, you can't see anything but what you want.

That's why it is helpful, in all honesty, to face whether either of you has one of these problems:

—Feels they are missing out on their youth.

—Feels like an outsider with the other person's friends.

—Feels too much a product of their own time.

—Feels the other person is jealous, selfish, or untrustworthy.

Or,

—You disagree about children.

—You feel embarrassed about the age difference.

—You can't live in the other person's social circle because its members are too mature or too immature.

And finally,

The absolute deal-breaker: the other person has been or is cheating on you.

Three principles describe successful age gap couples.

1. Both are mature adults.

2. Both are all-in, with no reservations.

3. Both feel a connection which makes them right for each other.

The following couple illustrates the three principles.

My husband and I are a May–December couple. We met when I was 25 and he was 46. We have a wonderful relationship in every way.

THE YOUNG WOMAN'S GUIDE TO OLDER MEN

I admire the maturity he brings to our relationship, and he admires my youthful energy that helps keep him young. He introduced me to music and movies that were not part of my generation, and I taught him the importance of an open mind when it comes to new fads, culture, and technology.

Our families and friends have accepted us. They tell us we radiate love. Our philosophy is there are so few chances in life to be truly happy, so by God, if you see a chance to be happy, even if only for a short while, grab on to it with both hands and never let it go.

Neither I nor my husband have been married before or have any children. I am now 31, my husband is 52, and we've been married five years. We are expecting our first child. We are both extremely excited! However, my husband is concerned about raising a child at his age. Where can we find information about support groups for older dads?

Morgan

The main point in this chapter

There are three principles of age gap relationships:

Both parties must be mature adults. Both must be all-in, without reservation. Both must feel the connection that makes them right for each other.

The second most important point

If you are not sure it's love, let time go by. Are the feelings growing? Are the feelings lasting? Are the feelings strong? If something niggles at you and tells you not to go forward, wait. Because that's not how love feels.

Chapter Twenty-Three

Hard Work

I am 20 and in a relationship with a man 16 years older than me. Don't you think there are situations where things might be best for people to work out? And maybe they worked through it, and now are even happier.

Alexis, age 20

We hope Alexis won't enter a relationship thinking she can work on it, because that is a clear sign something is awry.

The idea of relationships-as-work goes back 100 years, to the 1920s. The historian Kristin Celello even wrote a book about it, called *Making Marriage Work*.[1]

As Celello explains, psychologists, and those who would soon be called marriage counselors, promoted this idea: Just as there are natural sciences, so there is a "relationship science" that can fix couples' problems. In short, anyone who wanted a successful relationship could have it *if they worked hard enough*. Kristin Celello refers to this notion as a "shift from religious authority to scientific authority" as a way to keep marriages together.[2]

What has always intrigued us is that, at the time, there was no actual research evidence to support this claim.

Celello says, "Much of the appeal of the working at marriage formula was its universality; any married person who aspired to have a successful marriage could do so by trying hard enough."[3] And she points out, those who promoted the idea of hard work were lowering the bar, as if to say, having a relationship you can "work on" is good enough.

Relationships-as-work implies none of us can be genuine, none of us can be spontaneous, and none of us can be ourselves. Toss out your authentic self. Live by manipulation and calculation. The idea makes as much sense as saying, to have friends, you must do the hard work of friendship.

It's not even clear what the work is supposed to be. Helping with the dishes? Complimenting her every day? Boosting his ego?

We view the relationships-as-work idea as a century-old bromide, not as a guide for action. It's the psychological equivalent of throwing salt over your left shoulder. The assumption is that we are all interchangeable parts, and it almost doesn't matter who you are with. You can make any relationship work. That is nonsense.

None of the age gap couples who belong together speak like that to us. In their letters, they never mention they "worked" at it.

There is an even deeper problem with "relationships as work."

As the sociologist Melvin Lerner demonstrated in the 1970s, the idea work guarantees the reward is a cognitive trap.[4] It takes advantage of a built-in flaw in human reasoning. It is like saying the key to success with an internet startup or a new restaurant is hard work. But most people in those fields work hard and fail.

People want to believe if they do the work, they will get the reward. But that isn't true. Well-meaning people think, "I'm a good person. I can do the work." But a more realistic attitude is, "Life can be hard, and the right partner will make it far easier."

The main point in this chapter

Thinking you can hard-work a relationship into success is a mental trap.

The second most important point

Relationships-as-work assumes you can't find someone you can be yourself with.

Chapter Twenty-Four

A Scale

Earlier, we mentioned that age gap relationships follow a sliding scale. An age difference inappropriate at one age, may not matter at another.

We visualize an age gap scale looking like this:

NoNoNo – Iffy – YesYesYes – Iffy – NoNoNo

The left side of the scale, NoNoNo, refers to those who are too young for a significant age gap relationship. That is usually the female. When we get to those near adulthood, we pass from the No zone to the Iffy zone. It is not clear if people in this zone have the maturity for a lasting relationship, because there's no firm line between adolescence and adulthood.

In the middle of the scale, YesYesYes, are adults who understand what they are getting into and are old enough to decide for themselves. They are followed by another Iffy zone, where the two adults may be turning a blind eye to the problems between them.

At the far right end of the scale, NoNoNo, we think of Anna Nicole Smith and J. Howard Marshall. Smith, a former Playboy model, married Marshall, a billionaire 63 years her senior.[1] A wedding photo shows a vibrant Smith standing next to a shriveled man in a wheelchair. Marshall, 89 at the time, died a year later, triggering a nasty fight over his assets.

A scale like this is not an iron measure, except at the extremes. Typically, on the left end of the scale, the female is too young, while on the right end, the male is too old.

Chapter Twenty-Five

Summing Up

We began this book talking about our aloneness in the universe and about our need for love. We end in the same place.

Our self seeks another self. Not just any self, but the right self.

There must be a balance between the two people, despite the age gap. Both must be mature. That means, among other things, understanding what being together will be like.

WAYNE & TAMARA MITCHELL

In Jefferson County, Montana, there is a geological formation called Ringing Rocks. Tap a rock with a hammer and it chimes. Remove it from where it belongs, and it thuds.

That's something like a man and a woman who belong together. They resonate in each other's presence.

In the letters we get from couples who fit together, they consistently mention only one thing. The *natural connection* they have.

Looking back on her life, Jan said, "What a ride it was. If there were ever two people who completed two halves of a whole, it was us." Morgan, married for five years to a man 21 years her senior, said, "Our families and friends tell us we radiate love."

We cannot guarantee how your age gap relationship will turn out.

But youth and experience can be in love with each other, because each has something the other lacks.

About Wayne & Tamara

For over 20 years, Wayne & Tamara Mitchell have written the advice column *Direct Answers.* The column has appeared in newspapers in more than a dozen countries.

As one reader wrote, "I found your column several years ago by accident, but read it regularly. You provide the most clear, concise, gender neutral and useful answers."

Wayne & Tamara are also the authors of *Cheating in a Nutshell, What Infidelity Does to The Victim*.

WAYNE & TAMARA MITCHELL

Acknowledgments

Tamara's Acknowledgement

Special words of thanks to Nadya Yayla and Diane Handrick. Their constructive critiques and sharing of life experiences sharpened our focus on this topic.

Wayne's Acknowledgement

Five regular readers of *Direct Answers* made thoughtful comments about age difference relationships. Thanks to Jane Terry, Philip Knoll, Moses Ajwang', Sandra Stout, and Susan Voskuil.

Endnotes

Chapter 5 Why?

1. Conroy-Beam, Daniel, and David M. Buss. "Why Is Age so Important in Human Mating? Evolved Age Preferences and Their Influences on Multiple Mating Behaviors." *Evolutionary Behavioral Sciences* 13, no. 2 (2019): 127–57

2. An excellent article for non-professionals is: Stöppler, Melissa Conrad. "Puberty Definition, Stages, Duration, Signs for Boys & Girls." *MedicineNet.Com*, May 2, 2022.

3. A classic paper trying to blend the findings of social psychology and evolutionary psychology is: Kenrick, Douglas T., and Richard C. Keefe. "Age Preferences in Mates Reflect Sex Differences in Human Reproductive Strategies." *Behavioral and Brain Sciences* 15, no. 01 (1992): 75–91

4. Conroy-Beam and Buss previously cited. See also, Buss, David. "Sex Differences in Human Mate Preferences: Evolutionary Hypotheses Tested in 37 Cultures." *Behavioral and Brain Sciences* 12, no. 1 (1989): 1–14

5. Ninety-nine percent... Taylor, Paul D, and Aaron O'Dea. *A History of Life in 100 Fossils*. London: Natural History Museum, 2014. From the Introduction.

We almost lost... Sinclair, David, and Matthew D LaPlante. *Lifespan: Why We Age - and Why We Don't Have To*. New York: Atria, 2019. 220

6. For simplicity, we lump three things under reproductive potential: fecundity, the probability of conception per sex act; reproductive value, future reproductive capacity; and fertility, the actual birthrate by age, which is a proxy for fecundity. See Conroy-Beam and Buss, above.

7. David Buss. *The Evolution of Desire: Strategies of Human Mating*. New York: Basic Books, 2016. 7-8

8. Ibid. 349

Chapter 6 Love Is Common, True Love Is Rare

1. David Buss. "What Do You Believe Is True Even Though You Cannot Prove It?" *Edge.org*. https://www.edge.org/responses/what-do-you-believe-is-true-even-though-you-cannot-prove-it. Accessed January 4, 2023.

Chapter 7 The One Thing They Talk About

1. Rusbult, Caryl, Christopher Agnew, and Ximena Arriaga. "The Investment Model of Commitment Processes." *Purdue Univ., Department of Psychological Sciences Faculty Publications, Paper 26*, 2011.

2. Acevedo, Bianca, Arthur Aron, Helen Fisher, and Lucy Brown. "Neural Correlates of Long-Term Intense Romantic Love." Social Cognitive and Affective Neuroscience 7, no. 2 (January 5, 2011): 145–59

Chapter 10 The Ages of a Woman

1. Somerville, Leah H. "Searching for Signatures of Brain Maturity: What Are We Searching For?" Neuron 92, no. 6 (2016): 1164–1167.

Neuroscientists label people 18-22 as an "emerging adult." They are betwixt and between, part adolescent and part adult.

2. Armor, David A. and Shelley E. Taylor. "When Predictions Fail: The Dilemma of Unrealistic Optimism." In Gilovich, Thomas, Dale Griffin, and Daniel Kahneman (eds.). *Heuristics and Biases: The Psychology of Intuitive Judgment*. New York: Cambridge University Press, 2002.

See also, Lynn A. Baker and Robert E. Emery. "When Every Relationship Is Above Average." Law and Human Behavior 17 (1993): 439-450.

Suffer divorce... In 2012, psychologist Jeffrey Jensen Arnett conducted a nationwide poll and reported that 86% of 18-

to 29-year-olds surveyed expect to have a marriage that will last a lifetime. Arnett said, "It is striking to see how optimistic today's emerging adults are about their prospects for having a life-long marriage. They grow up knowing that half of marriages end in divorce, yet nearly all of them expect to be in the half that doesn't."

Jeffrey Jensen Arnett and Joseph Schwab. "The Clark University Poll of Emerging Adults." December 2012. PDF.

Chapter 11 How Now Brown Cow

1. The major exception is the continent of Africa, where the age gap may be much greater.See, Bhrolcháin, Máire Ní. "The Age Differences between Partners: A Matter of Female Choice?" in *Human Clocks: The Bio-Cultural Meanings of Age*, Claudine Sauvain-Dugerdil, Henri Leridon, and Nicholas Mascie-Taylor (eds.). Bern: Peter Lang, 2005.

2. Year 2014 taken for illustration. United Nations Economic Commission for Europe. "Mean Age of Men at Marriage." Https://W3.Unece.Org/PXWeb/En/Charts?IndicatorCode=300; "Mean Age of Women at Marriage." Https://W3.Unece.Org/PXWeb/En/Charts?IndicatorCode=303. Accessed March 22, 2020

3. All U. S. statistics from: U. S. Census Bureau. "Age Difference of US Married Couples." Current Population Survey, 2019 Annual Social and Economic Supplement. Table FG3, 2019.

Chapter 12 You've Got Daddy issues, Darling

1. Skentelbery, Sara G., and Darren M. Fowler. "Attachment Styles of Women-Younger Partners in Age-Gap Relationships." Evolutionary Behavioral Sciences 10, no. 2 (2016): 142–47

Chapter 13 Numbers

1. American Academy of Child and Adolescent Psychiatry. "Teen Brain: Behavior, Problem Solving, and Decision Making." *Aacap.Org. No 95*, September 2016.

Chapter 17 The Ideal Age Difference

1. Locker-Lampson, Frederick. *Patchwork*. London: Smith Elder, 1879.

2. DiDonato, Theresa. "Who Is Too Young or Too Old for You to Date?" *PsychologyToday.Com*, May 2, 2014.

3. Ibid.

4. EHarmony Editorial Team. "Does Age Matter in a Relationship?" *EHarmony.Co.Uk*, MAY 16, 2012. Accessed January 4, 2023.

5. Francis-Tan, Andrew, and Hugo M. Mialon. "'A Diamond Is Forever' and Other Fairy Tales: The Relationship between Wedding Expenses and Marriage Duration." *SSRN Electronic Journal*, September 15, 2014.

6. The data scientist is Randal Olson. As of July 28, 2020, a discussion and most of his graph can be found in Megan Garber's article in TheAtlantic.Com. All of the graph can

be found in Quentin Fottrell's article on Marketwatch.Com. Last time we checked, the graph and original description, if any, have been removed from the Olson site, though the date of the post remained unchanged.

Garber, Megan. "For a Lasting Marriage, Try Marrying Someone Your Own Age." *TheAtlantic.Com*, November 9, 2014.

Fottrell, Quentin. "The Bigger the Age Gap, the Shorter the Marriage." *Marketwatch.Com*, November 11, 2014.

7. Wilson, Ben, and Steve Smallwood. "Age Differences at Marriage and Divorce." In *Population Trends 132, Summer 2008*, 7–25. New York: Palgrave Macmillan, 2008.

8. Dutch Central Bureau of Statistics. "Relaties Meest Stabiel Bij Klein Leeftijdsverschil." *CBS.Nl*, June 13, 2019.

"Age, the Age Gap and Education All Impact Divorce Rates: CBS." *DutchNews.Nl*, June 13, 2019.

9. Gentleman, Jane, and Evelyn Park. "Age Differences of Married and Divorcing Couples." *Health Reports* 6, no. 2 (1994): 225–40. "...divorce rates are lowest when the husband is two to ten years older than the wife or when the magnitude of their age difference is extremely large. Furthermore, the chance of divorce is much higher when the wife is older than the husband..."

See also, Boyd, Monica, and Anne Li. "May-December: Canadians in Age-Discrepant Relationships." *Canadian Social Trends*, no. 70 (2003).

10. Lehmiller, Justin, and Christopher Agnew. "Commitment in Age-Gap Heterosexual Romantic Relationships: A Test of Evolutionary and Socio-Cultural Predictions." *Psychology of Women Quarterly* 32, no. 1 (2008): 74–82. By the same authors, "May-December Paradoxes: An Exploration of Age-Gap Relationships in Western Society." *Purdue Univ. Department of Psychological Sciences Faculty Publications, Paper 27*, 2011.

Chapter 20 How to Tell Family and Friends

1. Manning, Alan, and Nicole Amare. "Bad News First: How Optimal Directness Depends on What Is Negated." *IEEE International Professional Communication Conference (ProComm)*, 2017.

Christensen, Andrea. "Delivering Bad News? Don't Beat around the Bush." *BYU University Communications*, October 24, 2017.

2. Barbosa, Brenda. "This Is the Best Way to Deliver Bad News According to Science." *Inc.Com*, October 28, 2017.

Chapter 21 Another Word About Telling

1. Barbosa, previously cited.

2. Stone, Douglas, Bruce Patton, and Sheila Heen. *Difficult Conversations: How to Discuss What Matters Most*. Kindle,

10th Anniversary Updated. New York: Penguin Books, 2010. From the Introduction.

3. Ibid. Chapter 6.

Chapter 24 Hard Work

1. Celello, Kristin. *Making Marriage Work : A History of Marriage and Divorce in the Twentieth-Century United States.* Chapel Hill: Univ Of North Carolina Press, 2012.

2. Ibid. 26

3. Ibid. 8

4. Lerner, Melvin. *Belief in a Just World : A Fundamental Delusion.* New York: Plenum, 1980. 31-36, 106

Our discussion of Lerner's work is found in: Mitchell, Wayne, and Tamara Mitchell. *Cheating in a Nutshell: What Infidelity Does to The Victim*. Third Ghost Press, 2019. Chapter 10.

Chapter 25 A Scale

1. Lee, Dan. "Paw Paw & Lady Love." *New York Magazine*, June 3, 2011.

www.ingramcontent.com/pod-product-compliance
Lightning Source LLC
Chambersburg PA
CBHW072037110526
44592CB00012B/1459